MW00613916

Finding
Your
Black Belt

How to Kick Ass in Your Own World

by
Karen Conover

Happy Living

Published in the United States by
Happy Living Books Independent Publishers
www.happyliving.com/books

Copyright 2018 by Karen Conover

Researched and written by Karen Conover
Edited by Kelly McKain
Cover Art by E.R.Canedo

All rights reserved. Without limiting the rights under the copyright reserved above, no part of this publication may be reproduced, stored in, or introduced into a retrieval system, or transmitted in any form or by any means (electronic, mechanical, photocopying, recording, or otherwise) without prior written permission.

For permission requests, please contact:
hello@happyliving.com

Printed in the United States of America

ISBN: 9780999477120

Other Books by Happy Living

www.happyliving.com/books

Inspiring Women (2017)
by Matt Gersper

The Greener The Grass (2017)
by Scott Barry

Love Letters from the Grave (2016)
by Dr. Paul Gersper

Turning Inspiration into Action (2016)
by Matt Gersper

The Belief Road Map (2016)
by Matt Gersper and Kaileen Elise Sues

Join Our Community

Join our community to stay informed of upcoming books, promotions, and weekly inspiration from Happy Living!

We are on a mission to improve the health and wellbeing of the world, one person at a time.

Our blog is packed full of ideas for living with health, abundance, and compassion.

Go to www.happyliving.com to sign up for your free membership.

License Notes

Thank you for purchasing this book. This book is licensed for your personal enjoyment only. This book may not be re-sold or given away to other people. If you would like to share this book with others, please purchase an additional copy for each recipient. Thank you for respecting copyright and licensing law.

For permission requests, please contact: hello@happyliving.com

Disclaimer

This book is a work of nonfiction. The events and experiences detailed herein are real and faithfully rendered to the best of the author's abilities. Some names, identities, and circumstances may have been changed to protect the privacy and anonymity of the various individuals involved.

Please note that this book and all content from Karen Conover and KC's Family Tae Kwon Do contributors represents personal opinions based on experience. Before making any changes to your lifestyle or exercise routines, please consult a physician or other appropriate expert.

For my son and daughter, Chris and Kirsten. Being witness to you finding your own black belts and using those tools as you continue the cycle of learning that is life, has been my greatest honor. I have learned the most in my life from you and you inspire me. I love you.

For my kindest love, Marcus. Your honest heart is a gift to everyone who knows you and I am so grateful for every day with you. I love you.

FOREWARD

by Matt Gersper

It doesn't matter who you are, how old you are, what gender you are, or how much money or social status you have, you can succeed in Tae Kwon Do and in life if you develop a black belt attitude, cultivate your character and set your mind to never, *ever* give up. Tae Kwon Do is a wonderful example of the Japanese concept, Kaizen, which I believe is a foundational practice for success in any and every aspect of life. Kaizen is the idea that small incremental improvements add up over time to yield big results. It's simple, it's powerful, and it works.

Tae Kwon Do is a daily practice of learning certain attitudes, principles, and of course, physical movements. It starts out slow, easy, and simple - learning to bow onto the dojo floor while saying "Honesty, Respect, Friendship". It then becomes more complicated; the white belt attitude is Honesty and the form requires ten movements to be memorized and correctly executed. Later still, you come to the hard-to-believe-you-could-ever-do-it elements: the last form prior to black belt has more than forty movements that must be performed precisely and in perfect order - not surprisingly it's attitude is Perseverance.

Tae Kwon Do is a community of people helping each other become better at their art. The rules, norms, cultural status, and burdens of life are left outside when you walk through the studio doors. A new order is established. The business executive, stay-at-home mom, and troubled fourth-grader are equals in the white belt class—and all of them bow and say "yes-ma'am" to the twelve-year-old black belt. As they advance together through the belts, this unlikely trio inevitably develops the strong bond of teammates. It happens naturally as they face fears together, help each other along, and celebrate successes in a *genuine* culture of honesty, respect and friendship. It's a beautiful thing to witness.

Tae Kwon Do is a repeatable process of personal development. Physical movements are taught, practiced, and mastered. Character traits are studied and embraced. Fears are faced—in public tests—and overcome. Success is celebrated across the entire community. Confidence builds. Body strengthens. Mind toughens. The next belt comes. Ever more complex physical movements are taught, practiced, and mastered. The process repeats, forever and ever. The student becomes stronger. The student becomes wiser. The student grows into a master and teaches the students who come after.

That is Tae Kwon Do. That is Kaizen. That is life!

Master Karen Conover has created a school and a system to teach, test, and graduate students with strategies and best practices required to succeed in life—perhaps the greatest of which is to never, ever give up. She has helped hundreds of people in her Cottonwood, Arizona community achieve better health, happiness, and success in their lives, and you'll hear directly from a few of them in the pages that follow.

This book is Master Conover's way of reaching beyond the geographical limit of her school to share the lessons of her martial arts experience and inspire you to honestly, respectfully, diligently, and with discipline, try your very best in all you do in life. And when you do, to celebrate and completely accept yourself. This is the continuous process of self-improvement. This is the daily practice of Kaizen. This is how to find your black belt and start kicking ass in your world. How do you start? Well, my dear reader, you just begin by turning the page.

I wish you every success in life that you can imagine. With Karen Conover on your side, that's just what you'll get.

With love,

Matt

Table of Contents

INTRODUCTION

"Everyone has their own best." - Christopher Conover

As the Head Instructor of a busy tae kwon do school, I am in the very privileged position of being in a front row seat when my students find their black belt. The time at which they make this amazing discovery varies. Sometimes their black belt is found during the final push in the training that leads up to the big test, sometimes it happens at a moment during the test itself, and sometimes it happens the instant that belt is tied around their waist. As a Master of martial arts, I am so fortunate to watch, and be a part of, someone's great achievement. I get to witness the epiphany, the light bulb moment, so to speak. Being awarded their black belt is what happens on the outside; the moment they *find* their black belt is what happens on the inside.

I know what you're thinking, that earning a martial arts black belt makes someone a lethal weapon, a top athlete, a ninja, Bruce Lee and an ass kicker all at the same time. That's what I thought too, when I started martial arts twenty years ago. Along my way to earning four levels of black belt, I have found that achieving one means many things, and it's different for each person who earns it. Something else that not many people realize is that black belt is really only the beginning of a martial arts journey. The most important thing that I've learned about the black belt is that it transcends training in martial arts. It's an attitude for anyone and everyone to embody in taking on life's challenges, whether you're eight or eighty, an athlete or someone who has never owned a pair of running shoes.

My plan for this book is to share with you what it's like to attain an actual martial arts black belt, to highlight the life lessons that can be learned throughout that process, and to help you to reflect on how you might utilize those lessons in your own life, martial artist or not. The book will have three sections, which focus on Black Belt Attitude, Black Belt Character, and Black Belt Mindset respectively. I have such gratitude for the training and teaching experiences that I've had in martial arts and so do many students who have been privileged to experience that black belt journey with me. This is why I will share some of their touching words as well – excerpts from the speeches they've delivered just before earning their black belt rank. I hope our messages inspire you to adapt the Black Belt Philosophy in your own world and lead you to kick ass in your own life!

ATTAINING A MARTIAL ARTS BLACK BELT

Starting a martial arts journey doesn't usually include any expectation of great things. Yes, there is always the promise that if one works hard, then the black belt will come. But I really didn't think that applied to me. I was going to be Bruce Lee? *Pshhht, I don't think so. But this is fun and way cooler than the gym, so I'm gonna keep going!* The usual beginnings in martial arts are completely awkward and unsure. You walk into a studio full of people who seem to know a ton more than you and then your limits of comfort are tested right from the first day: Can you stand on one foot for longer than ten seconds and snap out a kick, then remain on one foot for another ten seconds in control and without wobbling? Can you complete five pushups, then ten, then twenty, even though you've never done sports or fitness? Can you memorize a pattern of moves, which foot goes where and which hand is next to chop or punch? Can you handle someone grabbing you tight, as you listen and learn the escape? It can be overwhelming to be a beginner at anything, especially when coming to it as an adult, and martial arts are no exception.

The way your typical martial arts school works is like this: there is a progression of belts from white belt through various color belts that lead to a black belt. Each belt signifies a completion or mastery of certain techniques and requirements. In my school's case, there was a balanced kick, a bunch of combinations or techniques, a form or kata, sparring drills and self-defense moves that had to be learned for each belt. There are ten belts prior to black. A typical timeline gets you there in four years after acute study, training, practice and tests.

I started martial arts as an adult at age twenty-eight, right after the birth of my first child. Call it a workout-get-back-into-shape plan where someone with a black belt cracks the whip. I was a soccer athlete and musician in high school and college, so pushups and memorization have never been a problem for me in martial arts. I wasn't afraid to perform either. But confidence, that was what I didn't have. I always questioned whether I was good enough and definitely didn't have a belief in myself in this new arena.

My first great moment in martial arts was earning my gold belt (which is the next belt after white). It felt like I'd earned a black belt. *Woohoo! I did something!* The graduation to my gold belt happened to be the same day that others earned their black belts and the big Master came for the test. I remember feeling awkward and unsure. He even corrected me on my bow when I approached him to receive my belt. I will never forget what he talked about that day: a black belt is a white belt who never quit. Ah! It seemed so simple, how to get there. Just keep going. Perseverance. That moment, I think, was when I actually 'found MY black belt'. I found my confidence and the belief that I could attain it. From that point on, nothing could stop me. I ended up earning my first-degree black belt six months after the birth of my second child and in a timeline of three and a half years.

Climbing the Mountain

Six months prior to the black belt test for the school I lead, training is ramped up and things get serious. Your life becomes all about martial arts and attaining the black belt. Your schedule is maxed out with long training for at least four evenings per week, plus a team cross-training 5k run every weekend. Did I say run? Well, that's not exactly it. It's a trail run-hike-mountain climb. Just when you thought you'd be out on the land on crisp early mornings for an hour or so – BAM – you look straight up and have to get to the top of a half-mile incline that feels like a death march, right after running through hill and dale for two miles. Except... with this mountain, you have to run it. And... you have to complete this grueling course in under an hour.

It'd be awesome to finish at the top of the hill and look around, but the finish line is actually back down at the bottom. The way down is treacherous - loose rock, ditches and divots to avoid – all while hoping your new sneakers have enough grippies on the bottom to keep you from sliding all the way down. Fear, panic and exhaustion gradually turn into confidence, success, and elation, and, as time goes on, we become conditioned to the task and better at conquering it. It's pretty amazing how perspective changes when you 'just do it', as the Nike slogan says. Every challenge can be overcome with attitude and practice.

We've successfully graduated dozens of black belts, all of whom completed the running challenge within the one-hour time limit. Were all of them runners and supreme athletes? Nope. Some were overweight, some lame with questionable strength in their knees, some pushing senior citizenship, some young kids who never heard the words 'push through the pain' and who, until that point, were conditioned to stop when things got hard, they became out of breath, or felt their muscles tire. But everyone, eventually, did it. Why? Attitude and practice, along with great doses of encouragement and teamwork. You see, this is a huge part in finding success: Maintaining the can-do attitude and applying consistent effort.

Surrounding yourself with people who believe in you and cheer you on is also vital to your success. This can manifest in the form of classmates, peers, parents, friends, or our children. They help us to stay focused and positive during the times where we waver in our confidence and drive. For me, it's my parents' voices that keep me going. Both of them are now gone, but the memory of hearing Mom say, "Go, Karey. Hustle," (from my soccer playing days) or "Go get 'em, Karen," from my Dad, echoes in the back of my mind. My Dad recently passed away and that "go get 'em" was the last communication we ever had. It was when he found out I was going to write this book – my first book. Anything is possible with this kind of support in our lives, so surround yourself with those who lift you up.

Black Belt Training and Testing Standards

The actual testing for black belt is pretty extreme. It's a three-day long examination. On Day One you have the Curriculum Qualifier. This is the day where you have to complete all of the material you've ever learned since white belt in one sitting, judged at the highest of standards. Kicks must be head level, stances must be low, punches and chops must be sharp. That holding your leg up for ten seconds you did at white belt? Try doing it for one minute, without any bobbling around. That's the standard here. You can hear a pin drop in this part of the test, which is closed to all but two supporters from your family. There is a panel of judges that include every black belt from within the school that has come before you, plus the Master.

Day Two brings the Conditioning Qualifier. Start with the mountain run at 8am, then get locked into the studio for eight more hours of calisthenics, pushups, kicking, sparring, self-defense and anything else the Instructors throw at you. The object here is to not quit, but just to keep going. No matter what. The challenge of being the Instructor in this moment is to push people further than they ever imagined they could go, without their bodies physically quitting or breaking their spirit. I have always had smiles at the end of the day on my tests. Bumps, bruises and sometimes blood too, yes, but all worth it for having overcome the challenge.

On Day Three it's the Black Belt Stage Test and Graduation. One might think the word Graduation makes this day feel better. But it really doesn't. It's still a test. Guest Masters arrive and watch you go through your paces on a stage, this time with an expectant audience also watching you. You're now required to give a speech in front of this huge group of people as the lights blare down into your eyes, microphone in hand. 'What Martial Arts Has Done for Me' is the topic. You're probably feeling the fear of public speaking suffered by so many, and listed as America's number one fear, above death and loneliness. Giving that speech is thrown into the mix of earning and finding a black belt too, because it is, after all and ultimately, about overcoming fear.

'What has your martial arts experience done for you?' is the question, and you would be amazed at the answers. The youngest black belt I've ever promoted was eight years old and the oldest was 50-something. They both had to answer this question. Being asked to ponder your life and the martial arts you've dedicated every moment to over the last several years, and then share this with the world? Wow, what a moment of truth for the soul.

The cool thing about this task is that it covers the gamut of human experience: we conquer a common fear; we get to be honest with ourselves and others; we get to reflect on ourselves – where we've come from, where we are and where we are going. We express gratitude. And in doing this practice, it helps us to grow even more. It is important to celebrate ourselves and this one final task helps us to do just that. In this moment, there is usually not a dry eye in the house. The audience members become witness to one's breakthrough of finding a black belt as the speech goes on and it's incredibly powerful. It is the pinnacle moment and the last thing that happens before having the black belt tied around a candidate's waist.

It is because of sharing these amazing experiences with my students, seeing them work hard and sweat, and then listening to these words from their speeches, that I do what I do. I'll be introducing you to some of them, throughout the next three sections, as I elaborate on the life lessons that impacted each of them most. They inspire me, they make me proud, and they help me learn from their experience, as I hope will be the same for you.

So, what does it take to get through all of this and receive your black belt? Well, I've seen a lot of black belts in my twenty years. Some are amazing athletes who can kick over their head and who impress as one would expect with their toned physique and clear talent for this kind of movement. There are those who don't look the part or who can't quite hold those kicks up. There are those who are even uncoordinated. One might wonder… isn't there a set standard for the black belt? Well, yes. And, sort of. And, no. You see, a black belt is often times what you make of it. Of course, you have to complete physical requirements and let's face it, some folks are better at that than others. You have to be able to defend yourself and have successfully completed the training and testing requirements. But I like to remember what my son, who is only fourteen and already an Instructor said: "Everyone has their own best." Because THAT is the standard for black belt, really and truly. If you have found your best and have learned the lessons of discipline, respect, perseverance and confidence, then it's your time.

A Student Speaks...
TRESSA WIMER

Two years since earning her first-degree black belt, Tressa is currently training for her second-degree black belt, has become a certified fitness Instructor, and also an Instructor of TKD. She is currently the front desk manager at our studio and loves being in the position of supporting others in their black belt journey, all while watching her children grow up and thrive by her side in the TKD school.

> *"TKD has forever changed mine and my family's lives. It has shaped us into wiser people." -Tressa Wimer*

When I walked into the studio six years ago with my very excited seven-year-old, never did I expect this journey we were starting or that it would lead to me standing up here tonight. Soon after getting my son signed up, my two younger kids and I joined. I really wanted to be able to help my kids with the curriculum and reach my fitness goals. Well the funny thing about journeys is they're full of surprises - some that will give you inspiration, some that will give you strength to fight old demons and some that will give voice to unrealized dreams. I thought I was doing this to help my kids, yet they are the ones that have helped me with my forms and kicks. They inspire me daily with their abilities.

I've enjoyed so many special life moments thanks to this school. One of my oldest demons and biggest fights has been my weight. I have struggled most of my life trying to find that balance between healthy, skinny, fit and fat - trust me I have been all of them! In the past few years it has seemed every time I started making progress on getting to my health goals, life would give me a big ole speed bump and knock me out of the race. The last time, in fact, I actually gave up TKD for a little while, but you can't be a quitter when you have to be the example!

So, I made a choice to not quit and persevered through the aches and pains and fully committed myself. Since then I have lost 50 pounds!! I now have the right tools and knowledge to keep it off. And as for that voice of unrealized dreams, sometimes the simplest questions will bring out the most unexpected answers. When asked by Master Conover at our conditional black belt test what getting my black belt meant, my answer was simple - completion. I have accomplished something that not many can do. I now know I can be successful at anything I put my mind to. So, to wrap this long story up, TKD has forever changed mine and my family's lives. We live with more purpose, better discipline, happier hearts and stronger bodies. I think most of my teammates would agree with me that tonight and the last six months have been some of the most impactful times of our lives. It has shaped us into wiser people.

SECTION 1 - THE BLACK BELT ATTITUDE

Let's start here... "You earned your black belt!" is like a metaphor for: you've gotten that promotion or achieved that life goal. You're at the top of your game, you've made it! How many times have I found myself here? Many, and it feels great! You might even be at that moment right now in your life or career. After celebrating my magic moments both in martial arts and in my life, I always remind myself that being at the top is really just a new beginning, because of course there is always more.

Set New Goals

I thought when I started martial arts that it was about fitness and earning a black belt. There were always jokes and questions like, "Once you're a black belt, do you have to register yourself as a lethal weapon?" I truly didn't know the answer to this. (The answer is "No", by the way!) I also thought that earning a black belt was the pinnacle, the top, and the end of the road of Mastery. But it's really not. Just like when you get to the top of a mountain and look beyond, you see more mountains. Black belt and martial arts is the same. There's always another challenge out there waiting for you.

I teach my students that black belt is only the beginning, like earning a high school degree. You've got the basics down, now let's look further. This is the part where we have to become humble again and set new goals for ourselves - towards a second-degree black belt and beyond. I am currently a fourth-degree black belt and that comes with the title of Master. While that's fun, I'm still pretty humble with it, because while that might be equivalent to having gone on through a Bachelor's Degree, then a Master's Degree and maybe it's a little bit like a Doctoral Degree, every day I see and interact with those who have higher degrees than me. There are Grand Masters and those who have been teaching and running a school much longer than I have.

I don't know what those Grand Masters know, but I want to set a new goal to learn. And the theme that rings through this is my use of the Black Belt Attitude, so to speak. This is the attitude in which setting goals helps us rise to new challenges and new depth of understanding. Embracing the humility to learn, the confidence to believe in your next goal, the drive to practice it and make it happen, and the perseverance to never give up -- this is the learning cycle that is most important and one that we can all take with us beyond the practice of martial arts.

A Student Speaks...
RON ROMERO

Ron continues to train and instruct in TKD and is currently a second-degree black belt. He is a reading specialist at a local school and spends much of his time outside of work with his black belt wife and daughters. His journey to black belt included a knee injury at blue belt and subsequent surgery that could have made him quit, but rather, it became something to overcome on his path. His ability to never give up is an example to us all.

> *"You need to set goals for yourself if you're going to succeed in martial arts or anything that you do in life. Remember, take it in small steps." - Ron Romero*

Joining tae kwon do has been a very tough but rewarding experience. We learn and try to strive for concepts like honesty, respect and friendship. That means trying to do your best in everything and don't cheat yourself in or others in the things that you do. Respect is a term that we use in TKD and answer our instructors, classmates and others with a "Yes, ma'am" or a "yes, sir". We respect people and things in and out of the studio. Friendship comes as a result of being with people with the same goals and aspirations as you in martial arts. We met a lot of good people while in martial arts and you can say we truly have a family attitude toward each other. We also learn concepts like discipline, goals and trying your best. You need to set goals for yourself if you're going to succeed in martial arts or anything that you do in life. Remember, take it in small steps.

My first gi was a size seven now I am wearing a size five. When I first started, I couldn't do three push-ups and now I can do fifty. I could barely do ten sit ups now I can do one hundred. I have improved my flexibility, strength, endurance and overall health. When I first started I was diagnosed with diabetes, and high blood pressure. My medical lab numbers and results improved by taking martial arts. My doctor said, "Keep doing what you're doing." A lot of my fitness came from being accountable, that means showing up for class and practicing. We tend to keep each other accountable in classes and with our groups. If somebody is struggling with a form or combo, we will help and encourage them. If a person misses a class, we ask about them and check to see if they are ok. We also tend to push each other to make one another stretch, grow and to take us all out of own comfort zones. That is the only way you are going to succeed in martial arts, and in life.

I had a bump in the road during my journey. I blew out my patellar tendon in my knee when I was receiving my blue belt. I was giving a self-defense demonstration, and I felt embarrassed because I got injured during a belt graduation. I didn't know what to expect but unfortunately it was more serious than I expected. At the time of my injury, I felt the best physically and mentally for martial arts. I also knew that I was going to fall behind my belt class. By that time, I knew I wanted to go all the way and try to strive for my black belt. I wanted to have surgery as soon as possible because then the healing and rehabilitation process could start. The hardest part was keeping my leg in a straight leg brace for ten weeks. I wanted to get on the studio floor and participate with the class. But I knew I had to be patient. I knew it was going to require small steps to get back into shape and form.

Tae kwon do has done a lot for me and my family. We get to do an activity that has brought us closer together. I enjoy that my oldest daughter is turning out to be quite a great young lady. She is becoming a capable teacher and leader. I love training with my wife, too. We like to compete and push each other to become better. We have fun and call it marital counseling. It is neat to see her grow and get in shape. She's been an inspiration and 'rock' for me. My youngest has also grown a lot in her journey and we are definitely going to keep helping her to move forward. I hear a lot of people say they wish they could do martial arts. I hope to inspire people to feel that they *can* do it. People tell me that it's crazy taking martial arts at 45 years old, but it has been one of the best decisions that I have ever made. It's pushed me physically and mentally. It's gotten me in better shape and heath. I've met and befriended some great people. I don't know what the future holds in this journey but I know I don't want to stop. I want to keep getting in shape, learning new skills and pushing myself to get better. I know that being a black belt will take me to another level and I'm looking forward to that.

Take it to the Next Level

In reality we are all responsible for ourselves as grown-ups. We wake ourselves up, feed ourselves, shower, get dressed, go to work, pay our bills, take care of others, etc. There is no one there to help us. Congratulations, you've got the basics down. You have reached stage one in the game of life, or what we'd consider a first-degree black belt in martial arts: a point at which the basics are understood, performable and working for you.

Just like in martial arts, when you're moving to second and third degree black belts and beyond, life has its levels too. The next level after getting the basics down is to find a deeper understanding of them and to continue to get better at them. So, once you've got life rockin' and rolling, you start to ponder, what's next? Do I just continue this day in and day out existence or do I reach to for more?

You might seek out love, adventure, and significance to add value to life – it's the deeper meaning and the higher level of how we can 'do life'. Matt Gersper, founder of Happy Living[1], demonstrates this beautifully in his 'Seven Foundations of Health Pyramid'[2]. The base contains the four fitnesses (physical, mental, spiritual, financial), which is like life's basics. Then, you build on that with love and adventure. Finally, and at the peak, you have significance. Like martial arts, it really is continuing your basics, but finding gratitude and purpose in a different way as you go along.

Gather a Team around You

Finding more in yourself is work that can only be done by you. No one can stand up there and throw kicks and punches for you at a black belt test either. It's yours to own and kick ass with. Life isn't a team sport. Black belt isn't a team sport. Or...is it? I'm here to tell you, life is both a team sport *and* a solo sport! We all have our individual responsibilities, but the people you surround yourself with are your team, and in turn, you are theirs. You have coaches, teachers and mentors; you have cheerleaders and supporters; you have teammates; life partners and co-workers. One responsibility that is completely yours is to pick your team from this crowd. You get to decide who gets to be around you. So, keep yourself in a positive environment with a team that helps you to grow and doesn't shut you down. If your work

28

environment is toxic, find places where you might explore positive changes by discussing with a supervisor. If your friendships are one-sided or bring you down, see if you can work through those things to keep yourself in healthy, fulfilling relationships. In martial arts, while only one can do the moves, there is always a team around encouraging your progress and high-fiving you when you find success. So, set yourself up in the best 'life dojo' you can.

A Student Speaks...
KIRSTEN CONOVER

After earning her black belt at age eleven, my daughter Kirsten went on to become one of the best TKD Instructors we have ever had at the school, a job she held all through middle school and high school. She is presently a third-degree black belt and is training for fourth-degree black belt, which she hopes to attain at or about the time she graduates from college. She is completing her Junior year as an Elementary Education Major and loves her part-time job as a math tutor.

> *"The most important thing are the friends I've made. They've been supporting me through this whole thing." - Kirsten Conover.*

Hi, my name is Kirsten Conover and I am eleven years old. I've earned 24 belts in my life time. Now, you might be thinking there aren't 24 belts, there are only eleven, but let me tell you my story of tae kwon do. I started as a Lil' Dragon at another martial arts school before this one. I was only four at the time and my mom (who is my Instructor now) started just after I was born! My dad started with me and we were the same belt for a while.

I grew up doing TKD, all through the Lil' Dragons to low brown belt. My parents then started a new studio and told my brother and me that we had to start all over there. It was REALLY hard for me, especially since I was almost a black belt. I decided to go and I had to start all the way over at white belt!

A few months later, the black belt test for my old school happened. My family was invited to their graduation and, of course, we went. It was a really sad time for me, as I watched all my friends graduate to black belt. I practically cried the entire time, but I got over it.

I've realized many good things have happened to me as a result of moving studios. For example, I am stronger, mentally and physically, than almost everyone at my school. I'm also fitter thanks to the extra time training and a lot better at sparring than I would have been, had I stayed there to pursue my black belt at such an early age. In fact, in January, I went to the state championships and almost won... in sparring, that's something I've never been good at!! The most important thing, though, are the friends I've made. They've been supporting me through this whole thing. I'd like to thank them for always believing in me, pushing me and helping me to know I can do whatever I set my mind to.

Finding Your Black Belt

SECTION 2 - THE BLACK BELT CHARACTER

Now that you're setting new goals and really taking things up a level, and you have a great team around you in your life dojo, it's time to explore what it means to have the Black Belt Character. You see, being a black belt is as much about character as it is attitude (or even kicking and punching!). Along the journey through the various colored belts all the way up to black, we study character traits that help us put the Black Belt Attitude into practice in a positive way. For example, we may set a goal to be aggressive and go for the point when sparring in the ring, but we can do this, and should do this, with respect for ourselves, our opponent and the judge. We also remind ourselves of the importance of character through the daily practice of bowing onto and off of the dojo floor while saying "Honesty, Respect, Friendship." You don't need to bow or even practice martial arts to incorporate character into your daily life, so let's move forward and study the lessons of each black belt character trait as my martial artists learn them, belt by belt, right from the student manual at my school. We will start with the 'No Belt' character trait and its definition per the manual and then

33

continue up in rank until we have reached black belt.

No Belt - Discipline and Self-Discipline

Good discipline is to do what you're told. Self-discipline is to do what needs to be done without having to be told.

Parents in our school love this part of the martial arts - helping kids to be obedient, which leads them on to become self-motivated with daily tasks, such as chores or homework. How can we use the qualities of discipline and self-discipline in our everyday lives? For one thing, let's take it into our jobs. Good discipline is a quality of one who supports the boss and does what is asked of them, without complaint or negativity about the tasks. Having self-discipline takes that up a notch because, this type of person completes tasks as they see a need, on their own accord, and in support of the direction and goals of the leadership. When we work on this level it shows the utmost respect for our team, our boss, and our work environment. I know that as a teacher, a boss, and an organizer of large martial arts events, fundraisers, and performances, I most value the people around me who see what needs doing and do it, without always having to ask for permission or direction. Our leadership teams in my martial arts school are excellent at working in this way and we get amazing things accomplished together.

A Student Speaks...
RACE ARMSTRONG

Race continues to train in tae kwon do and is gearing up for his second-degree black belt test. Despite his voice-from-the-past words you are about to read, where he shares that running is a challenge, two years later he is now a talented cross-country athlete, as well as an accomplished pianist and an advocate for kids with autism.

> *"TKD has taught me how to be a leader." – Race Armstrong*

Hi my name is Race, I'm twelve years old, and I'm a fifth grader in Connections Academy. I came to learn TKD and to this school because I wanted to be a ninja. My mom and dad wanted to find a place where I would be safe and happy - at school I was having a hard time because of my autism. We wanted a place where I could make lots of friends, focus on balance and my attention span, and learn cool stuff. We wanted to help me with my autism. On my first day, I met Ms. Kathy and Mr. Chad. They taught me how to bow onto the floor saying, "Honesty, Respect, Friendship." They also taught me to balance my kicks, yell loud, and work hard. Watching Mr. Chad fly through the air and climb the walls and wave masters like Spider Man made me want to become a black belt. I knew, right from the beginning, that I would be a black belt someday.

TKD has also taught me how to work hard, even when it's doing things that aren't so fun for me. Like running and belt stretch. When I started at this school I had no balance. I couldn't stand on one leg or even skip. Now I can hold a belt stretch on one leg for one minute. I am not the best at it, but I practice every day and my dad reminds me of a scripture that tells about weak things becoming strong if we work hard and have faith. I know that is why I can do better belt stretches now.

TKD has taught me how to be a leader. My mom had a hard time when she was pregnant with my baby brother and Dad works two jobs. I had to help out a lot more in our house. Being in this school helped me help my family better and I'm grateful.

White Belt – Honesty
To tell the truth to yourself and others.

We've been taught to tell the truth and never lie since childhood, right? So, it seems obvious that we know this is important, but let's look at it a little closer. The telling the truth to others part is the easiest – telling the truth prevents us from having to remember a web of lies, and far more importantly, keeps us open to others. It means we are presenting our authentic self, inside and out, nothing to hide. It really keeps the anxieties of life down and it's the right thing to do, of course. But what about that 'tell the truth to yourself' thing? What does THAT mean? Well, we know what it isn't, right? It isn't those justifications we make for everything. It isn't the- "If I drink this Diet Pepsi, then it's ok to have a second dessert"-type of inner-speak. But our true self reminds us of what is right and we should try to listen to that, more often than not, in order to put honesty with ourselves into practice. Integrity is a type of honesty that means to do what is right even when no one is watching. Do the right thing for yourself because *you* are watching and you are the most important part of the equation.

Gold Belt – Respect

Treat others the way you want to be treated.
Many have been taught that respect is the golden rule. Have you really looked at yourself around this one? There are so many instances where we disrespect others and don't even know it or (ahem!) where we lie to ourselves in order to justify the behavior. For instance, those amazing tools that are glued to our hands every day – smart phones. Have you ever spoken to someone who was head down busy on their phone only for them to give some generic reply that makes you think they heard, but really you know they're not paying attention? You'd want them to put the phone down, come over, look you in the eye and complete the conversation or communication with you, right? Or at least you'd want them to provide a respectful response. For example, I do a lot of business on my phone through messaging and social media. I have to really work hard to ensure I'm being respectful and paying attention to the people who are around me in the real world. It's not that difficult to give a "please hold on, I'm working here, just a minute" reply in a respectful way. Have you ever done this to someone? Clearly, I have and I remind myself to treat others in the way I'd like to be treated and I work hard to be better at it. It's essentially karma. What you put out into the world is what comes back to you. We should

also look at the places where we might be respectful to some, but not to others. Judgement of others is a big form of disrespect. We put people into a box and label them without even knowing them. So, put your best foot forward in your treatment of others, no matter who they are, or what their background, politics, race, gender, age, identity, etc. This is practicing true respect in our lives. In martial arts, respect is also practiced through good sportsmanship – win or lose, be gracious and grateful. That is true respect.

A Student Speaks...
CODY ZELLNER

Cody is a young man who makes me especially proud as I remember the days when he trained with us. When he started, he was a pre-teen already getting into trouble and doing poorly in school, definitely headed down an undesirable path. He completely turned around during the time he trained. His years in TKD helped him to become a leader, a straight-A student, and a great role model and instructor to the students he taught. He earned his first-degree black belt at age fourteen and went on to attain a second-degree black belt.

"Without sportsmanship I wouldn't be standing here right now. I'd be in the backseat somewhere crying with a ditch not done." - Cody Zellner

During my time at the TKD school, I have learned many things. Three of those things are confidence, self-discipline, and sportsmanship. Without sportsmanship I wouldn't be standing here right now. I'd be in the backseat somewhere crying with a ditch not done. Without self-discipline, I wouldn't be here right now either. Because of practice at home, I learn self-discipline and that's also how I keep my grades up. Without confidence, I definitely wouldn't be delivering my speech right now. I would like to thank everybody for being here because I really do enjoy your company.

I would like to thank all the black belt candidates for always being there for me and all of my family who came down. I would also like to thank my instructors: Mr. Conover for inspiring me by being 40 and still landing a back flip. He's also as tall as me. I realize if he's this tall and if he's 40, then I can do a backflip. I would also like to thank Mrs. Conover, for always being there and giving me the right information when I do something wrong. I stopped that. I was bad at school and made a bad choice that got my green belt taken away. That's been a long time. Luckily, I don't do that anymore. I know that my TKD friends are always there when I need them.

Orange Belt – Friendship
Friendship gives strength to my community.

Honesty creates a respectful interplay between people and can result in strong bonds of friendship. Great friends create an environment of support and positivity. It is why like folks gather with like folks. The best of relationships where people attract one another, are the ones rooted in honesty and respect - it really does build strong communities. Oftentimes, relationships can be rooted in negativity and hate: the group of girls who gather after someone's breakup, and all they do is talk trash about the other person; the hate groups around the globe who are focused on negativity and disrespect. There tends to be more focus put on negativity than positive. Many of us remember negative things that have happened to us, more so than the good stuff. As a teacher, I try to remember this. I motivate through an abundance of positive praise, rather than through negative discipline. I also surround myself with positive friendships.

Green Belt – Flexibility

The ability to stretch your muscles for TKD. The ability to 'go with the flow' when plans change.

The biggest excuse I hear from adults who might like to try martial arts but feel they may not be cut out for it is: "I'm too out of shape and am not flexible." That's just fear talking. When we talk about flexibility in martial arts, this includes the proper stretching of our muscles pre-and-post-workout in order to help our bodies avoid injury and to better ourselves for the movements. This is something that anyone can attain and improve with practice over time.

However, flexibility has another important meaning: the ability to go with the flow if plans change. While this is a great concept for the children in our programs to learn, it has so many applications to our everyday lives as grown-ups out there in the world too. Being flexible with the things that may interrupt our plans, job flows, or family time by events such as illnesses, car trouble, a new boss, or a cranky child can really help us to stay calm and avoid stress. Plans change and that's ok. Sometimes new plans lead us to ideas or experiences that we never would have thought of otherwise.

Case in point... I am a planner, down to the finest detail, so flexibility is a huge lesson for me. My family once took a trip with friends to Disneyland. We had it all planned out, right down to which rides to go to first and which to leave until later. I had a map and itinerary all set. When we got there, the kids definitely wanted to go where their energy led them. So, we ended up going down a tunneled path (unplanned) and in that area there was a Disney employee stopping people to give them Dream Fast Passes. Our entire group ended up getting gold star treatment and a special pass to use for the rest of the day, all because I relented and let go. This example shows that letting go plays a huge part in being flexible and developing happiness in all of our moments, and sometimes pays off in fun and magical ways.

A Student Speaks...
JUNIOR QUEEN

Junior earned his TKD black belt at the age of 49, is a former TKD Instructor, and is presently a Senior Manager for eBay. While he no longer actively trains in TKD, he takes his black belt with him in life. He frequently delivers motivational speeches for his sales teams using the black belt philosophy, along with challenging his employees to break a board as a means toward gaining confidence, focus and direction. He is married to his high school sweetheart and they have one son. The whole family trained in TKD together.

> *"Now, over three years in and here I stand, sporting a new 32-inch waist at 168-lbs, with excellent blood pressure and healthier than I've been in years. Oh, and I can reverse hook kick at head height, that's always cool." - Junior Queen*

Well, I was told the best way to overcome your fear of public speaking was to imagine your audience... umm... you know... in swimsuits, yes swimsuits. That should work...

The day I first walked into TKD I was much heavier and a little out of shape - ok a lot out of shape. But despite my 36-inch waist, I wasn't there for me, at least that's what I thought. I actually came to see if my son was as interested in martial arts as I had been at his age. He was. Months later I was digging through old boxes looking for a black belt that I had earned in my early twenties. I thought this would be a good time to show my son what I had achieved and how martial arts had shaped my life. The following week I squeezed into that belt designed for a much smaller Junior and made my way to the free trial class at TKD. At the end of the class I removed my belt, folded it, and approached the counter where Master Conover was standing. She has a confident smile on her face as if she knew I was looking to sign up. I stood in front of her, holding my black belt, and before I knew it, she nabbed it out of my hands and said, "Welcome to KC's Family TKD, you'll get this back when I tie a KC's black belt around your waist." Strangely...it was exactly what I had been thinking!

A year into the program, and I had a 34-inch waist and was feeling better than I'd felt in years. I found myself saying "yes, ma'am" to a thirteen-year-old black belt as she ordered me to do pushups in class. Two and a half years in and I got to watch as my son earned his black belt, a very proud moment for his mom and me. Now I'm doing pushups and saying "yes, sir" to my own son. Ya, great, thanks!

But seriously, three years in and I've lost a ton of weight. My blood pressure, although it was never bad, was lower than ever and my cardio was equally as good. At that point, my wife joined the school where we greatly enjoyed the extra time together. Now, over three years in and here I stand, imagining all of you in your swimsuits, of course, giving a speech after earning my KC's TKD black belt, sporting a new 32-inch waist at 168-lbs, with excellent blood pressure and healthier than I've been in years. Oh, and I can reverse hook kick at head height, that's always cool. But mostly, I have improved my health and I'm spending quality time with my family doing something we all enjoy. So, there it is... what tae kwon do has done for me.

Purple Belt - Confidence
I believe in myself.

The sad fact is that those who lack basic self-confidence will struggle to achieve their goals and ambitions, even though this is in no way their 'fault'. You have to believe in yourself and in your goals to excel, and the martial arts teach strength and self-defense, both of which lead to self-confidence. "There's no confidence like self-defense confidence," Roland Osborne[3], an Instructor that I emulate and admire, always says. By the nature of the martial arts belt progression through baby steps, where you never quit, all the way through to a black belt, confidence builds with each success. It builds when you or someone else recognizes that you've been successful at something.

In martial arts, we have an instructor, or a belt, or a stripe on our belt as an outward symbol to validate the success and help reaffirm your belief in the goal. But what about those times when there isn't an outside reward? True confidence comes when we, ourselves, value and see the intrinsic reward of the activity in which we find ourselves. In my observation, the most confident people are those who are happy and secure with the process and not completely focused on only the end results. The end results are important for goal setting, but "I believe in myself" is really all about being happy with who we are, in this moment.

Blue Belt - Timing and Punctuality

Timing is the ability to score a point at the precise moment. Punctuality is to be on time.

Without timing a martial artist would never hit their mark. It's also true that we have to be in the right place and in the right timing for some of our moments in life. Five or six years ago, I sat down at a table with a tae kwon do parent at a fundraiser pancake breakfast, as I would normally do to connect and chat with people at events. The timing of choosing that moment led me to make a business and personal connection with the founder of Happy Living, Matt Gersper, and was one that helped me to reassess my life goals, my business strategies and ultimately led to the writing and publishing of this book. There's a little bit of luck in there too. But mostly, there is patience involved in good timing, and in waiting for the right moment, just like in earning a black belt, which doesn't come just because you want it and want it now. It takes patience and time and when that time is right, then it happens for those who never gave up.

Red Belt - Balance and Rationale

Balance gives us centered techniques in TKD and centered minds in life. Rationale is the reason behind our choices.

We talk about balance a lot in martial arts, particularly in tae kwon do. We perform lots of kicking which requires balance from our core. Our life requires that as well. Ever heard the phrase 'too much of a good thing'? It's true. Our ability to balance our activities from work to family and everything in between helps to keep us focused and patient. By living balanced lives, we avoid burn out and can maintain a healthy level of inspiration and energy in everything we do. If we're striving for balance in our lives, we must always ask ourselves why we do what we do and reflect from time to time.

Rationale is the 'why' question behind what we do. There must always be a valid reason for doing what we do, and it must always come from a positive place. Why do I train in martial arts? Because I see how much value it has given me, my children and all those who've trained with me. It keeps me healthy and inspired. Why do I spend a lot of time on Facebook? Because it helps me to network for my business, share positive stories and connect with friends from far away. Finally, as you explore the balance in your life and the rationale behind why you do the things you do, don't forget to always allow time for yourself.

A Student Speaks...
BONNIE POND

Bonnie earned her black belt alongside her husband and her two children. She continues to train in TKD and has recently made the decision to challenge herself by making plans to test for a second-degree black belt. She regularly explores coming out of her comfort zone, most recently by agreeing to learn 'tricking' (a combination of martial arts kicks with gymnastics) so she can become a better instructor. She is an occupational therapist by trade. Read her speech closely for the 'aha!' moment at which she 'found her blackbelt'.

"Choosing to commit to the goal of earning my black belt made all the difference in the world! My consistency in practicing and my desire to improve came much easier." - Bonnie Pond

How can I tell you how I feel about a journey that I never planned on taking? The journey was supposed to be about our seven-year-old twins, not about me. I don't remember wanting to take classes nor do I remember signing myself up or even earning my white belt. What I do remember is

My brain said, "Of course you can do this."

My body said, "Yeah, right!"

My heart said, "It will be so good for the family."

My nerves said, "You don't have the time or the money!"

Seriously, I was in conflict with myself. And so, the journey began.

My biggest struggle in the beginner belts was learning how to balance work, home and tae kwon do. Many days I would get the kids or myself to class late or get to class without a uniform, belt or piece of sparring equipment. I would arrive to many classes unprepared. The patience and perseverance from instructors and G-Team friends really helped me return week after week. The words of encouragement by phone, mail and Facebook from my instructors were exactly what I needed to stick it out.

Don't let me mislead you though. Many days were a blast and I felt great! The school had become a family within my own family. I had seen friends come and go, I saw relationships begin and end, celebrated new lives and milestones and grieved tragedies. I have even enjoyed a special Halloween wedding for two of our black belts.

The journey towards intermediate and advanced belts came with mixed emotions. I was ready to begin learning musical forms but dreaded the sparing and self-defense. My learning curve was vertical. Really. At 40+ years old I had to learn to be thrown on the ground and to not run away from somebody who wanted to hit me. This old dog did not want to learn new tricks! Learning to balance on one foot with a belt wrapped around the other was not on my agenda.

The physical challenges of tae kwon do, tendonitis, random joint pain or a racing heartbeat were nothing in comparison to the challenge of only letting Bonnie Pond onto the mat. Who knew it would be so hard to leave my roles as a wife, mother and occupational therapist off of the tae kwon do floor? Somewhere along the TKD journey, which I never intended to have, TKD has helped me pay attention to Bonnie Pond.

The day I told Master Conover that I had decided to move ahead to earn my black belt in 2016 was the day I was finally 'all in'. Choosing to commit to this goal made all the difference in the world! My consistency in practicing and my desire to improve came much easier.

Over the last five years I have been wildly blessed by people who, at white belt, I was yet to know and are now my closest friends. I have wonderful family memories and am healthier and happier than I have ever been. As it turns out, my journey with this TKD school has become one of the best seasons of my life!

Low Brown Belt – Attitude
Present yourself positively.

This is one of my favorite martial arts lessons. We use it all the time as parents to our children too. I often hear parents at our school say to their kids that we get to 'choose' our attitude. But how often do you see adults forgetting to choose their attitude? Have you seen that person swept into social media drama that has gone on to ruin their day? What about after reading the news, particularly political news? If it upsets you, how do you respond? Oh yes, of course it can trigger emotion, and sometimes that emotion is as strong as anger, fear, resentment or even hate, but do you fly off the handle in reaction and then do nothing to restore your inner harmony and balance?

Personally, I try very hard to choose my attitude in these moments. There are days when I see red after reading such things, and those are the times at which I'm tested most. As much as I can, I choose to deal with my feelings about something quickly and then move on to more positive pursuits. In this world of a 24/7 news cycle, it's common to encounter this daily and I recommend that, if you find yourself in this position (or in any situation where your attitude is tested), you take a breath, express gratitude for the good things that you can and then decide how you respond to the challenge, moving forward with positivity. In my job, I have lots of challenging moments and a responsibility to lead a team, smile with customer service, and capture the attention of students in an inspiring way. I can't bring negativity along for that ride. I'm willing to guess that none of us can afford to do so in our workplaces, and it certainly isn't healthy to do that in our home life either. So, onwards and upwards with a positive attitude is always a great choice.

High Brown Belt - Perseverance
To never give up, even when things get tough.

Some of the hardest challenges I've faced in my life had nothing to do with those put before me at black belt tests. Going through an unwanted divorce after twenty years of marriage, for example. Bringing foster children into my home, loving them and parenting each according to their unique needs. Becoming suddenly dependent on my martial arts school business to provide a living for me. The deaths of my parents, both before I turned 50. I'm sure you can relate to these kind of life challenges and have faced your own. The key is to use that black belt attitude of perseverance. Or, in the wise words of Dory from Finding Nemo, 'just keep swimming'[4]. You will find yourself where you need to be, if you just keep going.

Focus – Bonus Skill
Pay attention from beginning to end.

It's a simple enough concept - pay attention from beginning to end. One way that we develop focus in martial arts is when we practice a form. A form is a set choreography with a number of moves you have to demonstrate. The white belt form has ten steps. The last form prior to black belt has over 40 steps to remember. We need to pay attention to what we are doing, without being distracted by our own thoughts or what's going on around us, in order to be successful at completing the form. Life is the same, we don't want to be distracted. Developing our ability to zone in on our goal is key in meeting it, or we lose sight of it along the way. Pay attention to what matters, let go of what doesn't and you will find yourself focused on meeting your goals.

A Student Speaks...
ANDREA VARELA

Three years after delivering her black belt speech, Andrea is now a second-degree black belt, fourteen years old and a confident martial arts instructor to students aged four through adults. Here's what she has to say today: "Earning my black belt, and the years after, have definitely changed my life. I'm currently in eighth grade, a member of the volleyball team and a straight-A student. Being an instructor and black belt has given me more confidence and has taught me the value of honesty, respect, and friendship in all aspects of my life."

> *"There will be bumps in life, but none of them will stop me from achieving my goals." – Andrea Varela*

Tae Kwon Do has definitely balanced my life. I started TKD when I was seven years old. I am now eleven. At the time I started I knew it was a dream come true because I didn't think I'd get the chance to participate in martial arts in the first place, let alone eventually go for black belt. During this process I have definitely made a lot of friends. They are always there to pick me back up when I fall to the floor, they are always encouraging me to never give up and continue fighting for that dream. The instructors have definitely helped me during this process. I would like to thank you, Mr. Junior - my sparring and self-defense has definitely improved because of you. I'm not gonna lie, I hated you every time I got a kick to my head, and then I learned that every kick was making me stronger and teaching me how to be a stronger sparrer. Your words of encouragement will always be a part of my life.

Miss Kirsten, I would like to thank you for all the focus and techniques that you have taught me, you have been one of my inspirations since day one. I love the way you teach and always encourage others to never give up on their dream, that anyone is capable of living their dream. Not only are you a wonderful teacher, but you are also a great friend. I'd also like to thank Master Conover. You have definitely pushed me to the edge of the cliff, but not off. To be honest, I thought about quitting so many times, but you were always there to say the right words to keep me focused on my goal of finishing this dream that started on day one. Thank you for the hard, fun and challenging exercises that you have thrown in our path. And last, but never least, I would like to thank the most important people in my life. The ones who are always there to clean my tears every time I was hurting and you have always been supportive in this journey – my parents. I love you. Thank you for all the things that you have helped me with to be able to achieve my goal. And thank you, Grandma and Grandpa, for being the best supportive persons in this dream.

Getting a black belt is a symbol that I am capable of accomplishing anything that I set my mind to, that even when I'm tired after a long day I can still get up the following day and run a marathon. TKD and all of my friends and family have helped me get to this point using little steps. It's like when you are a baby – you first learn to crawl, then walk, but most important you get to run. I remember when I first started, I believed that I could only do 30 pushups. Then I got to 40, then 50, I think now I'm at 100, but it's the ability to believe that I can do it that matters most – that I can do whatever I want to do.

When I started TKD, I was going through a really hard time in my life, but I learned that being scared and hiding under a blanket would not help me or take me anywhere. I opened myself to believe that tae kwon do was my second home and that everyone around me were my new family. They helped me to recover my life and start a new chapter. They pushed me like an actual sibling would do, but also held me when I needed someone to talk to.

TKD and our school are very inspirational. They don't only help us to achieve our goals, but also to make new goals, to fight for them and to never give up. They teach us how to defend ourselves. And most importantly they teach us about friendship and honesty. They also help you to become a better person and a great student. Most importantly, though, they teach you to be someone to look up to. What I have also learned from TKD is that there will be bumps in life, but none of them will stop me from achieving my goals.

Tae kwon do has been a big part of my life. I have experienced the best times of my life in this journey, four long years. It seems long but at the same time it seems like yesterday when I received my white belt. I remember when I gave that carnation to my mom at my white belt graduation and told her that it would be a beautiful rose at my black belt graduation. Now look at me four years later. I grew like the carnation into the rose. I'm here proving to everyone that I did it, that this journey finally became reality. For everyone that didn't believe in me, I can prove to you that everything is possible – that if I did it, anyone else can. I am the second one in the entire family to get a black belt and I know we are not going to be the last ones.

I hope to pass on everything I've learned to other people, not only at my TKD school, but also to everyone around me. I want to let them know that I've gone through everything they are going through and hopefully, by looking at me and what I've accomplished, through dedication and hard work, it will inspire them to keep training and pushing forward. I hope to not only inspire my little brother, but also the Lil' Dragons. It was an honor to become part of the Leadership Team, and having the opportunity to help little kids was the best that has happened in my life. They looked at me with such interest. That helped me even more to continue on this path. Their little smiles and effort showed me that no matter how old you are, if you keep on trying, anything is possible. One of the things that I have learned about being on the Leadership Team is that 'A good leader always leads by example'.

SECTION 3 – THE BLACK BELT MINDSET

The Power of Mindset

So, you want to kick ass in life. Is that what got you reading this book? Great job on coming this far! There really is no secret to kicking ass, only success strategies and best practices. Think of the Black Belt Attitude and the life skill character traits we study in martial arts, and that you just read about, as my success strategies in life. They can become yours, too, if you apply them with purpose. I realize that not all of us have an interest in martial arts or want to be martial artists ourselves. I even recognize that all the people who study at my school might not want to be martial artists for their whole lives. This is precisely why the most important goal I have for my students is to be principled, confident and driven people (who can defend themselves). That way, they take the Black Belt Attitude, Character and Mindset out into the world.

Let's go back to the black belt character traits – Discipline, Self-Discipline, Honesty, Integrity, Respect, Friendship, Flexibility,

Confidence, Balance, Timing, Attitude, and Perseverance. You don't just decide one day you are going to incorporate all these things into your life and bam, you're a better person. It's a daily practice that slowly builds and benefits you over time, like martial arts. The more you mindfully practice these traits, the easier it becomes to live them.

So I can't say it's a quick fix. What I can say is that in 20 years of practicing these traits, I am a better person for it. I am driven in my job, yet also compassionate and respectful. I am open and honest with people and that develops respectful friendships and business relationships. I am confident in my world and that creates a solid foundation for those who follow me as a leader. I try new things and am not afraid to fail. I always believe in myself, and my big ideas, and never give up. In fact, it's what gave me the inspiration to write this book! Once the idea took hold, nothing could stop me from putting my fingers to the keyboard. I go above and beyond to help people. Frankly, in this world it feels really great to be nice. To be kind. I keep it positive on social media and in my everyday life. Do I slip up? Of course! Am I perfect? Nope. But I know what I want and strive for it as best I can.

So, how do you start this practice? Well, you just begin. You might consider your activities or your job or your home life and write about each character trait. Or pick a word or two to focus on for the day. For example, *today I am going to focus on Respect and Friendship*. Decide how you are going to go out there in the world and perform 'acts' of respect and friendship. Journal about it and then don't forget to come back to your journal to reflect on how you did. And have a celebration if you did a good job. It's ok to celebrate and share your achievement with your team. This spreads positivity and inspiration.

Ghandi's 'be the change' quote actually reads like this: "If we could change ourselves, the tendencies in the world would also change. As a man changes his own nature, so does the attitude of the world change towards him[5]." It really is our duty to be the best we can be, and to pursue excellence in all areas of our lives. Doing so inspires others to do the same and pretty soon the entire world around you, changes too. It's you creating your team, your happy place, and your best life all at the same time. It's you finding your black belt and kicking ass in the world with it.

A Student Speaks...
JADE OIUM

Jade was eleven when she earned her black belt. She left her training to pursue other athletic avenues (softball and volleyball) through middle school and high school. Jade is currently a senior in high school and will be graduating with honors in May of 2018. Jade has been accepted to and will be attending a top university nursing program this fall. The skills and principals she learned at TKD have shaped her into the amazing young lady she is today.

> *"I have learned that if you give a hundred percent in life you will get a hundred percent out of life." - Jade Oium*

Tae kwon do has taught me many things over the last four and a half years. One of the many things was that it helped me increase my physical ability. I have become much more physically fit and my stamina has improved. My flexibility has increased, too - this has made my stances lower, kicks higher and stretches wider. Being physically fit I am able to enjoy hikes in the woods or a game of chase at school. I love being able to participate in school sports or activities with ease.

Since joining the TKD school I have improved

my mental abilities as well. I have memorized forms starting at white belt all the way to Exodus (the high brown belt form) and all the combinations. This has helped me with my memorization at school also. My grades are excellent because of the skills I have learned through TKD. I have the confidence to achieve my goals: there are no limits to what I can do because mentally I know I can!

I have grown emotionally since I began my training at TKD. I have always been taught to believe in myself while training for my black belt and I know I can do anything I put my mind to. The first time I attempted the black belt trail run at Grief Hill, I was afraid I could not do it, but now I know physically, mentally and emotionally that I can!

The focus that I have learned while training has helped me in school. I know when a challenge is placed before me that I will be able to complete it. I have become a responsible young lady because of what my parents have taught me and what TKD has required from me. I have learned that if you give a hundred percent in life you will get a hundred percent out of life.

TKD has helped me build my self-confidence. I learned during my black belt training that anything I put my mind to I can achieve.

Be Inspired

It's so important to be inspired in what you do and I hope these ideas inspire you. I have known many people who were great at their job and made a lot of money. One would think that's a major goal in life, right? Well, I also observed that they were very unhappy in their lives. They weren't inspired. We are taught to get an education, get a job, support yourself, buy the house, buy the car, take the vacation. They sought to find inspiration and happiness in 'living the life'. Work for the weekend, work for the paycheck and the payoff. But, are we taught to be happy? Maybe, if we're lucky. But not always. Here's where inspiration comes in. Most adults spend most of their waking time at their jobs. Wouldn't it make sense to have a job and spend time doing things that inspire you? Inspiration and joy in the process of our life is what truly makes us happy. I am so fortunate that my job is also my passion and my hobby. I am grateful that my family also enjoys my passion because we get to spend time together and we love it. Find areas in your life that inspire you, whether that be through work or play.

Everyone Has Their Own Best

If you're at the point where you're thinking about making changes in your life because of what you've been reading so far, you're probably also at the point where you're evaluating how you are doing in your life. Don't judge yourself too harshly. I'd like to go back to that quote at the beginning of the book that is attributed to my son... he was the highest ranking black belt in the school (beside myself), and a fourteen-year-old Instructor, when he said, "Everyone has their own best." He said this to a class that included kids and adults who were trying really hard at something that was very difficult. It was such a simple phrase, but very inspiring - so much so that one of the adults who heard it really took it in and told me how awesome it was to hear.

It's not easy being an adult or 'G-Teamer' (as we call ourselves) in a martial arts school that also trains athletic kids. There is so much self-doubt when you look around and see others doing what you cannot do so well. This lesson from a wise and kind teenage boy changed the mindset of a woman whose confidence was faltering, to one in which she accepted herself as trying her best. Celebrate and accept yourself if you honestly, respectfully, diligently, and with discipline, try your very best – it's the Black Belt Attitude at the highest level and it can be used in all things. It really does sum up what I have to say about others in their martial arts journey or in their life's journey. We do the best with what we know and that's ok.

Accept Yourself AND Strive for Excellence

We can always do better, and at the same time still celebrate who we are right now and how we are doing today. The quest for earning a black belt (and beyond) is really just a tangible goal which allows us to achieve excellence in our martial art. The great by-product is that it helps us to be excellent in all facets of our lives. We go into the world and show extreme politeness, respect, responsibility, courage, perseverance, and discipline in everything we do. Or, at least, we try our very best to. And if we sometimes fail to reach the high standards that we set for ourselves, we are honest with ourselves, dust ourselves off and try again.

Facing Fear is a Practice

The thought of transforming your life or making changes can be daunting. The first time I submitted a sample of writing to the

68

editor for this book, for example, I was a little bit frozen with fear. I hadn't turned in work for someone to evaluate since I was in college. I was definitely coming out of my comfort zone! Your comfort zone is your happy place. Your bubble. That cozy nook we like to keep ourselves in that feels familiar and warm. I admit it - I love my comfort zone. But what I love more is daring to step out of it. All of our learning and growth happens when we leave our comfort zone.

It's really interesting how we see that take effect in martial arts. I have taken a non-athletic bookworm of a mom to black belt. I have taken overweight smokers with bad knees and many years on them to black belt. Every day was a step out of their comfort zone. From the first martial arts class all the way to the end where they were challenged by a crowd in the ring for five minutes of sparring or self-defense. They just 'put one foot in front of the other' as Kris Kringle sang in Santa Claus is Comin' to Town[6]. With just one foot outside that comforting and easy place, they learned and were better for it.

I see so many people who shy away from trying new things because the thought of stepping out makes them nervous. I truly believe this is the exact reason why someone should dive headfirst into an activity that makes them feel this way. It's overcoming fear. Facing fear is a practice. If we practice it daily, then pretty soon fear and anxiety become less present in our everyday life. Go ahead and face a fear, step outside your comfort zone every day and see what happens. I dare you!

A Student Speaks...
SHERRI RUGGIERO

After earning her first-degree black belt and teaching cardio fitness classes, Sherri left TKD to study psychology, where she earned her PhD. She is presently a practicing psychologist and university professor. She continues to push herself through running daily and completing a yearly half-marathon. She strives to find opportunities to evolve herself through her interaction with people, physical activity, and learning. She frequently asks the patients she sees for psychotherapy, when they feel like giving up or a failure, "What is a black belt?" After giving them some time to contemplate this question she provides the answer, "A white belt that never gave up." People get it. She loves this metaphor.

"In each of us there are places we have never gone. Only by pressing the limits do you ever find them." -Dr. Joyce Brothers

My three-and-a-half year journey with TKD has been the vehicle for me to press my limits, and find those new and vital places within myself. I am so grateful to have walked this path with such a fine group of instructors and martial artists. We have learned from each other, supported one another through challenges, and have always been there to congratulate each other through the stages of earning our black belts. Now, here we are today to celebrate one another, witness each person's success, and share in a collective rite of passage.

I started this journey at the inception of the school with my family by my side... not knowing what to expect. There has been an incredible amount of growth, and transformation, even in the face of significant adversity. I would like to share with you some of what has made my experience at this studio so valuable. The effects of TKD in my life have encompassed not only the physical but have created shifts mentally and spiritually as well.

Physically, my body has become a well-practiced tool of this martial art. Tae kwon do has been a new outlet to employ my physical energies, develop new skills, and has taught me to perform purposeful movement. I believe that I have obtained the strength and skills required to perform this martial art in all its grace and beauty, as well as a means to protect myself physically if the situation were ever to arise.

Mentally, tae kwon do has given me focus, helped me to stay aware of my surroundings, and stay present in the moment. There is really no better practice for staying 'in-the-moment' than to be executing fast paced punches and kicks on command, reacting to attacks within a self-defense class, or feeling the surge of the 'fight-or-flight' mechanism kick in during a sparring match. I am now more present and prepared to handle the diverse challenges of life. I have had valuable practice at allowing my mind to create the outcomes I desire.

Spiritually, I see myself as having evolved into a space of acceptance, appreciation, and respect. I have had to embrace life events that have truly challenged the foundations of my world. One of the great gifts that TKD has given me is a respect for perseverance. I would never have imagined that I would be able to perform the required tasks of a black belt had I focused on the end product. I took each day, then each week, then each month and year one step at a time until I arrived to this point today. Large tasks, such as a obtaining a black belt, can sometimes seem too overwhelming to even begin. Perseverance is the quality that reminds us to stay in the moment, be concerned with what is in the here and now and allow the accumulation of these moments to culminate into something more.

So, in reflecting on the quote by Joyce Brothers it is easy to see that my limits have been adequately 'pressed', and those new and beautiful places have opened up inside of me. I feel as though I have revealed more of my true and powerful self. This is what TKD and this school have given me, and I appreciate it more than words can express.

Pay It Forward, Give It Back

When I tested for my fourth-degree black belt and the title of 'Master', I had to give a speech on 'What Being a Martial Arts Master Means to Me'. Now at this point in my career, I had been running two martial arts schools and had taught hundreds of students. My biggest reflection on the topic is that a Martial Arts Master is one who serves, or rather, continues to serve. We are taught in martial arts that the higher the rank, the more responsibility we have to help others. This give-back principle helps to keep ego in check. It's easy to feel 'high and mighty' once you look at the belt around your waist and compare it to others' of a lower rank. Ego is never a good thing. Confidence is great, but ego, no. So, to stay humble, we serve others and share our knowledge as appropriate. You can take this idea into your world, by thinking about what makes a great boss in the workplace. Is it the task master who tells everyone else what to do? Or is it the one who helps others to be inspired and do great work? I would hazard a guess that you'd say it's the inspirer and the one who makes everyone else feel they are a part of a team with the boss there as a resource, encourager and leader in the job.

I have definitely seen both kinds of boss in my life after working in restaurants, schools, real estate offices, and non-profits. In my personal experience, I have little recollection of the jobs where the boss was just a task master. I remember the bosses and the jobs where I was encouraged. It inspires me to be the same kind of boss and leader at my school. Just last week, a teenage employee and instructor told me a story of how she watched a kid her age working at a fast food restaurant, getting ordered around and demeaned in the job. It made her express to her mom that she was so grateful for the opportunity to do meaningful work that inspired her at the TKD school. Hearing this made me so grateful that I can provide opportunities for people that go well beyond a teen job. It's my give-back as a Martial Arts Master – to inspire and share what I know with my students, instructors and employees. I know that if I can do that, then the lessons will stick with folks for life and hopefully get paid forward. That's why I'm sharing it with you. The lessons I've learned through my martial arts experience can definitely benefit anyone and I'm happy to pass them along.

A Student Speaks...
JOHN KELLY

While John no longer trains in TKD, his time at the school was marked by being known as 'Big John' or 'Mr. John'. A hulking man of well over six feet tall, he exemplified respect by being extremely polite and a caring Instructor to his students after earning black belt. He has raised three sons, all of whom participated in TKD with him.

> *"TKD gives my sons and I a chance to be a positive influence on others." - John Kelly*

This speech is supposed to be about what the TKD school has done for me. This is (was) one of the hardest things I have had to do in my training for a black belt here at TKD. I really don't enjoy talking about myself and find it hard to do so. But I have set myself to the task of looking within to figure it out and put into words what it has done for me.

The first and perhaps easy thing to talk about is the physical. When I walked into TKD the first time with my boys, I was just an observer, watching them while they took class. Most of the time I just watched, occasionally talked with other parents, or with staff. One of those times I was talking with the staff, one of the instructors told me if I wasn't careful I would find myself joining and would eventually find myself all but living at the studio.

Well she was right. After a month of watching my boys, I joined myself. At the time I weighed 240lbs, and just six months prior to that I weighed 270lbs. I had already started the process of getting back into shape, after having a stern lecture and threats of all kinds of meds from my family doctor. Well after three and a half years, I have gotten down to and more importantly maintained my target weight and blood pressure. Now, TKD didn't get me to that weight - that is something I have done more than once, key phrase being 'more than once'. But what it has done is help me maintain it and stop the yoyo effect.

Well that was the easy part, but I know that the purpose of this speech is to talk about more than just the physical things TKD has done for me. So, this next part took a lot more thought. And what the school has done is to give me a chance to affect others for the better. A couple of months ago, another parent at the studio told me that while he had been thinking about joining himself for some time, one of the things that helped him decide was watching my two sons and I, at one of the belt graduations. This was a proud moment for me, because it showed that I was having a positive effect on others.

Even more important to me were two different events that took place just a few months ago. The first was with my son Jefferson, who sometimes has problems dealing with frustration. Well, a few weeks ago, he was given an attitude stripe. He had been working with Mr. Cody, and was having a difficult time, and getting frustrated, and per Mr. Cody, rather than get mad and quit, or get discouraged, he got determined and worked through it, good enough that Mr. Cody recognized this in front of the class for him.

The other instance came with my oldest son Larry. Larry helps teach the Lil' Dragons and kids' classes. And while it was always a good feeling to watch him working with them, an especially touching thing happened away from the studio. Larry and I had stopped by the grocery store on the way home after class one night. And while there, we ran into one of the Lil' Dragons who ran up to and hugged Larry telling him, "thanks Mr. Larry, I had fun today." I have always been proud of my son, but to see that a seventeen- year-old could have that positive an effect on a little one was a great feeling. So, to sum up, what TKD, has done for me: it gives my sons and I a chance to be a positive influence on others. I am the proud father of three great boys. Thank you.

CONCLUDING WORDS

In the past twenty years I have earned four tae kwon do black belts to tie around my waist. But it is through my study and experience that I've found that being good at the Black Belt Attitude, Character and Mindset is something that builds and evolves and changes with every experience that I have. It's like having a black belt test every day. One day an out-of-control five-year old might make me have to change up my entire lesson plan and test my flexibility. Another day an upset customer may test my ability to be respectful, patient and confident. It's a cycle of learning that never ends, and a practice, just like martial arts. No one can take away a black belt once it's earned and, while there are those who stop the practice of the physical movement of martial arts, it is my hope that anyone who has learned from me, including readers, continue the practice of Black Belt Attitude, Character and Mindset wherever their lives take them.

You might be wondering, "Karen, have you found your black belt yet?" To be truthful, some days my answer is a resounding "YES!" And on some more challenging days, I am unsure. But then a soft voice in my head always whispers, "Patience, practice, it's all in the timing, don't give up." Finding your black belt and the wisdom that comes with it will come through this practice of being your best. Exploring and implementing the Black Belt Attitude, Character and Mindset, as set out in this book, will certainly get you off to a great start. In my case, just writing this book has given me new focus, so keep at it each and every day and soon you'll have a rock-solid set of skills for getting the very most out of yourself and your life. It has certainly contributed to filling my every day with love, happiness, inspiration, significance and success, as I hope it does yours, too.

ABOUT THE AUTHOR

Karen Conover is an entrepreneur, educator, and fourth-degree Black Belt Tae Kwon Do Master. She holds a Master's Degree in Music Education and has 25+ years of experience teaching children in public and private schools, as well as adults in classroom, corporate and workshop settings.

Karen owns and runs KC's Family Tae Kwon Do[7] in Northern Arizona, and more than 150 students attend her school. She uses martial arts as a vehicle for improving lives, and she loves it. She is grateful to all of her martial arts teachers and other inspiring people who have helped her as a martial artist, instructor, and school owner, especially her main Instructor for the last ten years, Master Shanon Preston of Arizona's Best Karate[8].

Karen has four children, two biological and two fostered, of whom she is extremely proud and loves very much. She is currently making wedding plans with her fiancé, Marcus, a man who makes life interesting, delicious and fun for their whole family. She loves to travel, see live music, escape to the movie theater, and spend time with her closest of friends, whom she considers family.

You can follow Karen and her martial arts school on Facebook – "KC's Tae Kwon Do" or check out the website at www.kcfamilytkd.com.

REFERENCES

[1] Happy Living - www.happyliving.com

[2] Seven Foundations of Health Pyramid - https://www.happyliving.com/2014/11/07/seven-foundations-of-health/

[3] Roland Osborn, Founder of Hyper Martial Arts - www.hypermartialarts.com

[4] Finding Nemo, Movie, 2003, Original story by Andrew Stanton, Screenplay by Stanton, Peterson, & Reynolds

[5] Ghandi quote - https://quoteinvestigator.com/2017/10/23/be-change/

[6] Santa Claus is Coming to Town, TV Special, Written by Romero Muller, Produced by Rankin/Bass Productions

[7] KC's Family Tae Kwon Do – www.kcfamilytkd.com

[8] Arizona's Best Karate – www.tryfreekarate.com

JOIN US AT HAPPY LIVING

Be advised of upcoming books and updates from Happy Living! We are on a mission to improve the health and wellbeing of the world, one person at a time. Our blog is packed full of ideas for living with health, abundance, and compassion. Go to www.happyliving.com to sign up for your free membership.

Happy Living

THANK YOU!

Thank you for reading Finding Your Black Belt!

If you enjoyed this book, please leave a kind REVIEW on Amazon.com!

Wishing you every success in life that you can imagine...

Matt Gersper
matt@happyliving.com

Made in the USA
Columbia, SC
02 July 2020

12156081R00052